Table of Contents

Table of Contents 1

Introduction to Law and Justice 2

Law and Justice...5

The theories of justice...6

How far does the law achieve justice?...11

Procedural justice – legal institutions and process...11

Substantive justice – the legal rules..12

Revision 18

A general guide to revision 18

Revision of Law and Justice...18

Examination practice 20

A general guide to examination papers 20

Writing a discussion essay: staging the information logically 20

Examination practice for Law and Justice 21

Answers to self-test questions and tasks 24

Appendix: Abbreviations and acknowledgements 30

Introduction to Law and Justice

Unit 4C, concepts of law, is *synoptic*. This means it connects to your other areas of study, not just the substantive law, but the institutions and procedures. You will be expected to show your understanding of these by relating them to the various concepts of law. In this booklet, we cover 'Law and Justice'. You should also be able to relate this concept to more contemporary issues and you will find plenty of examples here.

The theory of law is called *jurisprudence*, and is a compulsory part of most law degrees. Many academics, philosophers and judges have written about the theory of law and justice, and there is much disagreement between them.

Examination tip

You are not expected to 'take sides' when discussing the various arguments. You may wish to state your own opinion but if you do, be sure to back this up with reference to the theorists and to relevant cases. The main thing when it comes to the examination is to have a clear focus and keep your answer centred on the specific question asked, i.e., keep your answer and examples relevant and, where possible, use one or two of the theorists to support what you say.

Many cases involve several different concepts so you will see cases from 'Law and Morals' repeated here and are likely to meet some of them again in the other concepts. Other than cases from the substantive law, e.g., crime, tort or contract, there are many contemporary issues which will involve these concepts of law, such as whether it is right to force-feed an anorexic, whether separating Siamese twins knowing one will die is morally justified, whether gays should have equal marriage rights to heterosexuals and many others.

Examination tip

It is useful to learn and fully understand cases that can be used across the Unit well, because you can use the same one in different questions – as long as you change the focus. For the higher mark bands, especially in 'Law and Morals' and 'Law and Justice' you should also refer to the theorists on the area to develop your points. You can also develop your point by arguing for or against the decision.

Example

We can look at how the case of **Brown** can be used to discuss each of the five concepts in Unit 4C AQA Law. This is a very brief outline, as you have not covered all these concepts. However, it should give you an idea of how you can use a case and then adapt and develop it to different situations – a bit like judges do with law.

Concept	Aspect of the case that relates to this concept	Mention of a theorist where possible
Law and Morals	Whether sexual violence in private should be regulated by law rather than purely a matter of morality	**Devlin** would say 'yes' because immoral acts undermine the fabric of society, even when done in private **Hart** would say 'no' because law and morals should be kept separate **Mill** might say 'yes' because he believed in non-interference in individual rights, but could say 'no' because he added 'unless doing so could harm others'
Law and Justice	Whether justice is achieved by imposing legal sanctions against certain behaviour even if it occurs in private	The above could be used again but also a **Utilitarian** would want to see the greatest benefit for the greatest number so could argue that this is achieved by banning the behaviour of the minority to protect society as a whole
Judicial Creativity	Earlier cases conflicted on whether consent was a defence to serious injuries, the majority indicated the ratio was that it was not	Where a *ratio* is unclear, later judges can select the most appropriate or can distinguish the case on the facts. **Professor Goodhard** said, *"It is by his choice of material facts that the judge creates law"* Arguably with such a serious crime Parliament rather than unelected judges should create the law
Fault	It was unclear whether the decision was based on the amount of harm or whether the harm was intentional	*Mens rea* is an important element of criminal law and where harm is committed with intent it should be penalised The acts had been consented to, so it is wrong that the law penalised the behaviour. Even though there was MR the consent defence should have succeeded
Balancing Conflicting Interests	The interests of the public to be protected from violence had to be balanced against the interests of the individuals to act as they pleased in private	**Devlin** would say that society had to be protected from evil, as did some of the judges in **Brown**. **Lord Lowry** said sadomasochism was *"not conducive to the welfare of society"*, and so a **Utilitarian** might agree with the decision. **Pound** believed that public and private interests should not be balanced against each other as the public interest will always prevail, as seen here

The tasks are intended to reinforce your learning so do these as you go along. The answers are at the end of the booklet. Some tasks may just ask you to jot down a few thoughts for use in an essay, so there are no answers to these, but keep your notes for revision and exam practice. I have included occasional quotes so use these too; they show that you know what judges have to say about the law.

A brief reminder: Criminal cases are usually in the form *R v the defendant*. It is acceptable to use just the name so if the case is **R v Miller** I have called it **Miller**. If another form is used, e.g., **DPP v Miller** I have used the full title, as you may want to look up the case for further information. Civil cases are between the *claimant* and the *defendant*, although you will see the word *'plaintiff'* in cases before 1999.

There is a list of some common abbreviations in the appendix at the end of the booklet.

Task 1

Mill argued that the law should not interfere in individual rights unless the individual's actions could harm others.

Do you think Mill would have agreed with the following laws?

> **the law against drinking and driving**
>
> **the law making the use of seat belts compulsory**

Law and Justice

"Everyone seems to have a view of the proper outcome. I am very well aware of the inevitability that our answer will be applauded by some but that as many will be offended by it"

Ward LJ

The meaning of justice

Many people see law and justice as the same thing but this not necessarily the case. It is quite possible to have unjust laws. It is also possible to have unjust outcomes from just laws. That said, in liberal democracies at least, it is the primary aim of any legal system to deliver justice. Unjust laws are likely to be challenged and may become unenforceable.

Example

The 'poll tax' law, brought into effect in the 1980s, meant that everyone paid the same local taxes regardless of how big a house they lived in. One person living in a large mansion paid less than a family of four in a one-bedroom flat, because the tax was based on the number of people in a property. It was widely thought that the tax was unjust and a huge number of people, from many different social groups, demonstrated against it. This demand for greater justice led to the law being changed, because the fact that so many people refused to pay it in protest against the injustice it caused meant that it had become unworkable.

So what is justice? A simple notion of justice is that of fairness – treating everyone equally. When you hear someone say "But that's not fair!" it usually means, "You aren't treating everyone the same." Equal rights have long been an area of contention, and protests against discrimination of various kinds have been around for centuries, e.g., the right of women to vote and later to be paid equally were fought for in the last century, along with the rights of people of different races and religious convictions not to be discriminated against. There are now laws against many types of discrimination and these have evolved over time.

Example

For decades, gays (and many other people who believed in equality) argued that gay couples should have the same rights as heterosexual couples. The **Civil Partnership Act 2004** gave more rights to same-sex couples, but there were still significant differences and several cases went to the **European Court of Human** Rights based on discrimination – gays were not being treated equally because they did not have the same rights as other couples. In 2014 when the **Marriage (Same Sex Couples) Act 2013**, came into force many felt justice had finally been achieved because rights had at last been equalised.

Justice can mean different things to different people. There are several theories on the subject. You should be able to discuss some of them.

Examination tip

Don't try to learn all of the theories outlined here. You won't have time to discuss many of them, so use ones that make sense to you. Your essay will be more confident and it will be easier for you to use examples. Two or three theories well illustrated with examples will earn more marks than a recitation of lots of theories without developing any of them.

Many books have been written by, and about, the people putting forward different theories. It is a good idea to try to read someone first-hand if possible. You will get a much better feel for what they mean than you will by merely reading *about* them. It is only possible here to give an outline of the main ones.

Natural Law

The Natural Law theory regards law as coming from a higher source. Laws are based on moral rules. The origins of Natural Law theories lie with **Aristotle** and **St Thomas Aquinas**.

Aristotle (384 – 322 BCE) said that moral rules come from Nature. We have 'natural' rights. He argued that the basis of justice is fairness, and that this takes two forms:

Distributive justice – the law acts to distribute benefits and burdens fairly throughout society. This can occur through various laws governing property rights, e.g., in the law of theft and contract.

Corrective justice – the law acts to correct attempts by individuals to disturb this fair distribution. In criminal law, confiscation, compensation and restitution are corrective sentences. In civil law, D pays compensation to correct any wrongdoing.

Example

Football is played by equal numbers on both sides, using the same pitch, the same ball and the same-sized goals. If one team's goal were smaller than the other team's goal, that would be a breach of *distributive justice* – it wouldn't be treating the teams fairly. When a player breaks the rules the referee, a type of judge, imposes sanctions, e.g., a penalty, free kick, red or yellow card etc. In this case, the referee is using *corrective justice* – trying to compensate one team for the offence of the other.

Saint Thomas Aquinas (1227 – 1274) said that moral rules come from God. We have 'God-given' rights. He suggested that any law which went against morality would not be just. If a law is not a just law, we need not obey it. This is because it is not a 'true' law. However, he also said that such a law should be obeyed if *not* obeying it would disrupt society. This is because that would not be in accordance with God's will either.

Many countries have a constitution which sets out certain rights. These are seen as a higher form of law. If a law were passed which conflicted with constitutional rights, it could be subject to challenge. Britain does not have a written constitution. However, the **Human Rights Act 1998** provides that the 'natural' rights set out in the **European Convention on Human Rights** are part of domestic law.

Positivism

Positivists have tried to find a more scientific way of describing law, without reference to morality. For positivists, law *may* be based on ideas of morality or justice, but these are not *necessary*. The validity of law is not affected by whether it is morally acceptable. Most positivist theories attempt to explain what law *is* rather than what it *ought* to be. Although this means that a law is valid even if it is unjust or immoral, it does not mean it has to be followed blindly. Most positivists acknowledge that there may be times when a law should not be obeyed. What they *do* say is that even though it is unjust, it is still *law*.

Two important Positivists are **Kelsen** and **Hart**.

Kelsen (1881 – 1973) felt it was impossible to define justice. He tried to provide a science of law which excluded any political or moral content. He based his theory on a set of 'legal norms'.

He saw law as a form of social control. The legal norm imposes duties or confers powers on officials to apply sanctions; an example is giving judges the power to impose sentences and provide remedies.

Hart (1907 – 1992) distinguished between 'procedural justice' and 'substantive justice'.

The first he called 'justice *according* to law' and this involves questions of whether the *legal process* is just. Examples would be having access to justice, the right to appeal and jury trials.

The second he called 'justice *of* the law' and this looks at whether the *law itself* is just. For example to be just a law would have to apply to everyone equally

To Hart, the law is based purely on rules and is separate from issues of morality.

Positivism is clearly opposed to Natural Law theories. For a positivist a bad law would still be valid and have to be obeyed. A Natural Law theorist would disagree. Nazi law is often used as an example. Positivists might say laws discriminating against Jewish people should be obeyed because they were validly made by those with authority to do so. Natural Law theorists would argue that law must follow some 'higher natural law' and that if it did not it would not be 'true' law. The segregation of African Americans in the USA and the apartheid laws of South Africa, are other examples.

Essay pointer

Parliamentary supremacy in the English legal system means that Parliament can make any law it likes. If Parliament passes an immoral law, no judge can say it isn't just and people don't have to obey it. This is not much of a problem in a democracy, as unfair laws will lead to protests, as with the poll tax referred to above. The law was valid even though unjust, but the protests led to change to a fairer system. In less democratic societies, it is more of a problem to achieve justice. If a government passes an unjust law, it will expect it to be obeyed.

Utilitarianism

Utilitarianism looks at the *consequences* of a law, and asks whether it benefits more people than it harms. If a law 'maximises happiness', i.e., increases the total happiness or welfare of a society, it is just. Utilitarianism is often simplified as 'the greatest good for the greatest number'. However, utility is not concerned with *equal* distribution of happiness, but with *total* happiness. It can therefore lead to injustice because if there are a few extremely happy people, then total happiness may be greater even if there are many slightly unhappy people. Utilitarianism focuses on the needs of society rather than the individual. It is in conflict with individual rights and freedoms and is criticised by libertarians, who see the rights of the individual as all-important.

Jeremy Bentham (1748-1832) was a Utilitarian. He had little time for individual rights in the sense of natural rights, which he referred to as *"nonsense on stilts"*. His Utilitarian theory was an attack on the Natural Law theory. He tried to produce a more scientific approach to justice. He suggested that law should be evaluated by reference to the principle of utility, and not by reference to a *"misguided belief"* in Natural Law and natural rights.

Example

A law is passed which bans smoking in public. A Utilitarian would argue that the rights of the majority to protection from health risks outweigh the rights of the individual to smoke because the 'greatest number' benefit from the ban. This law would therefore be just. Some years ago, when more people smoked, a Utilitarian might argue against such a law.

Essay pointer

The introduction of the **Human Rights Act 1998** increases the rights of individuals. Consider whether this is against the utilitarian theory. Arguably, it is not, because all of society benefits from certain rights being enshrined in law. Anti-terrorism laws are arguably for the greater good of society, to protect the majority against harm. A Utilitarian could therefore argue such laws are just because the ends justify the means. An argument against this would be that society itself is diminished by unfair laws which harm everyone.

Example

Prior to 2006, foreign nationals suspected of terrorism could be held indefinitely without either charge or trial. The Law Society said, *"We recognise the government has a difficult balancing act. But it is essential that emergency terror legislation protects the country without compromising the government's duty to uphold fairness and justice."* The **Terrorism Act 2006** removed the indefinite detention but allowed suspects to be held without charge for 28 days. This was increased to 42 days by the **Counter-Terrorism Act 2008**. The **Protection of Freedoms Act 2012** has reduced it to 14 days. This shows the difficulties of achieving justice for everyone. We all want to be safe, but few people want to live in a society that can lock people up without any charges being brought against them. Such laws are against natural law as they conflict with the fundamental rule that no one should be imprisoned without a fair trial.

John Stuart Mill (1806-1883) was a leading Utilitarian and is still influential today. Mill was also a libertarian and attempted to unite the ideas of Utilitarianism and individual rights. He had a minimalist approach to law, arguing that people should have the right to act unless exercising that right harmed others. Only then should the law interfere to restrict those rights.

Task 2

Choose a case and explain how it relates to law and justice, with reference to one or more of the theories.

Note that Utilitarianism and Positivism overlap.

> *Positivism separates legal rules (law) from social rules (morals).*
>
> *Utilitarianism focuses on the consequences of the rules.*

Economic theories

Many economic theories are modern alternatives to Utilitarianism. Traditionally, Utilitarianism looks at maximising happiness. Economic theories try to measure this in terms of material wealth. Three important economic theorists are Karl **Marx**, John **Rawls** and Robert **Nozick**.

Marx (1818 – 1883) believed that the law only served the ruling classes, those who *"own the means of production"*. He wanted to see distributive justice (remember Aristotle?): *"from each according to his ability, to each according to his needs"* and thought the state should intervene to redistribute wealth. Marx did not support *equal* distribution, but distribution according to ability and need. He did not address individual rights as he saw these as reducing the power of people to work together for change.

Rawls (1921 – 2002) argued that Utilitarianism was flawed because it failed to take account of the *"separateness of persons"*. His theory is based on what rules a group of individuals would choose in order to make their society just – what earlier writers had called a 'social contract'. Rawls added a new ingredient called the 'veil of ignorance'. This means that the individuals making the rules would not know who they were and so could not be influenced by self-interest. If people do not know whether they are rich or poor, young or old, male or female, Jews or Christians, able or disabled etc., then they will agree only to rules which would protect them *whatever* the circumstances. Such rules would therefore achieve justice. This theory of justice is Egalitarian, based on equality.

Nozick (1938 – 2002) argued that for a just society there should be minimal interference in people's lives by law and state. Although he too rejected the utilitarian argument, he did not agree with

Rawls that wealth should be redistributed. He argued that if people come by something fairly, then the law should not attempt any redistribution because that would interfere with people's rights to their property. *How* goods or wealth were distributed within society would be just, as long as everyone *received* their property in a just manner.

Example

When patients take their local Health Care Trust to court to challenge a decision not to prescribe a particular drug, the courts have to make a decision, and try to achieve justice. In many cases, the treatment is expensive and funds would be allocated from limited resources, possibly reducing the availability of drugs or treatment for other patients. In **R (on the application of Rogers) v Swindon NHS Primary Care Trust 2006**, the CA held that the trust should have considered the woman's request for treatment. The point was not that all treatment should be funded, but that the policy in relation to funding should be fairer and more transparent. A utilitarian would want the hospital resources distributed to provide the greatest benefit for the most people. Marx would want any such distribution to depend on the needs of the patient. Rawls would probably prefer an egalitarian approach, so that resources were shared equally. The problem is that resources are limited so not everyone will be satisfied.

Issues of this type arise daily in many areas where the state provides care. Hospitals, councils, schools and other organizations with limited resources face difficult economic decisions every day, and such decisions will often also involve arguments about how, or whether, justice can be achieved. The National Institute for Clinical Excellence (NICE) publicised a report on the issue in August 2008. This adopted a utilitarian approach and said that if drugs are too expensive the NHS should not have to provide them, even if they would prolong life. Spending too much on one patient may mean denying treatment to several others. The NICE approach may mean Health Care Trusts have a stronger argument against prescribing drugs such as Herceptin.

Task 3

*Read the case study on **Rogers** and answer the questions*

A woman took her local Health Care Trust to court for not supplying a new drug called Herceptin, shown to reduce the risk of recurrence of breast cancer. It cost £20,000 per year and was not yet available on the NHS. The Trust's policy was to refuse treatment unless there were exceptional circumstances, and an example of what might constitute exceptional circumstances given in court was that of a woman with a child. The CA held that exceptional circumstances should be based on clinical needs rather than personal matters and, whilst not ordering the Trust to fund treatment, held that the Trust's refusal to fund the Herceptin treatment on such grounds was illegal, the decision should be quashed and the policy reformulated. Justice demands that the policy should be fair and that the allocation of resources should be decided on clinical needs and not the personal circumstances of a patient. The CA's point in **Rogers** was not that all treatment should be funded, but that the policy in relation to funding should be fairer and more transparent.

> *Why did the CA quash the decision of the Trust not to provide treatment?*
>
> *What might a utilitarian think of this decision?*
>
> *How would the utilitarian argument affect the individual patient and what might Mill say about this type of problem?*

Should all Trusts be obliged by law to supply drugs if they will help someone stay alive, or should they be able to use the money to treat several other patients with more minor problems?

Should individual Trusts make their own decisions on a case-by-case basis, depending on available funds?

In a similar case to **Rogers**, brought in 2008, a challenge was made to the decision of many Primary Care Trusts not to fund the use of the drug Lucentis. This drug has been shown to improve the vision of people suffering from certain eye disorders which could lead to blindness. The challenge again failed. Hospitals and doctors with limited resources face these difficult economic issues every day and the cases raise several questions with no easy answers.

Should all Trusts be made to supply life-saving drugs, if so who will pay?

Should the Trust make the decision on a case-by-case basis, depending on available funds?

Should expensive treatment be refused so that the money can be used to treat several other patients with more minor problems?

Task 4

What should go in the right-hand column in this table?

What is the theory?

We believe that law is separate from morality. We base our understanding of the law on rules to be obeyed – what some call legal norms. A law may be unjust but it is still a law.	Our theory is described as
We are concerned to maximise happiness. Some of us reject individual rights but others believe that the law should only interfere if someone exercising a right harms others.	Our theory is described as
We believe law is closely linked to morality and that moral rules come from a higher authority than the law. Unjust law is not true law.	Our theory is described as

How far does the law achieve justice?

Refer to all areas of the law you have studied for ideas on the extent to which substantive legal rules, institutions and processes achieve justice. Ask yourself the following questions.

Is the legal system just (procedural justice)?

Is a particular law just (substantive justice)?

Here are a few starting points.

Justice requires that there is a system of independent tribunals for the administration of law and the resolution of disputes (what Hart called 'justice *according* to law'). This would include trial by jury, appointment and independence of judges, financing of court cases, sentencing, remedies, and so on.

You could discuss:

> *Improved access to advice and representation under the Access to Justice Act 1999*
>
> *Changes brought in by the Legal Aid, Sentencing and Punishment of Offenders Act 2012 (which mean the claimant now pays any 'success' fee, reducing the amount of compensation received). This will adversely affect those on a low income because compensation is supposed to be exactly that, money to compensate for the harm done. Any reduction means it won't do this*
>
> *The appeals system and juries to provide greater protection for D*
>
> *The Criminal Cases Review Commission set up in 1995 with the sole purpose of correcting injustice (as in Kennedy 2007). Its establishment is a clear acknowledgement by the state that injustices do occur. In February 2005, e.g., the Prime Minister issued a public apology to victims of what he called 'state injustice' such as the 'Guildford Four'*
>
> *Precedent is based on treating like cases alike which is fair; other rules of precedent can be used to avoid injustice caused by too strict an adherence to this rule, e.g.,*
>
> > *Crime: The use of the 1966 Practice Statement in Gemmell to overrule Caldwell*
> >
> > *Contract: Merritt distinguishing Balfour*
> >
> > *Tort: Setting a precedent in Donoghue*
>
> *Remedies and sentencing*

Remember Aristotle's *'corrective justice'*? Civil remedies aim to achieve justice by ensuring D compensates C for any wrongdoing. In sentencing, the aim is to achieve a just balance between the interests of society (deterrence and retribution) and the defendant (rehabilitation). Mitigating and aggravating factors can influence the judge to do what is just in the circumstances.

Substantive justice – the legal rules

How far does the law achieve justice in crime, contract and tort? (This is Hart's 'justice *of* the law'.) Here are a few ideas.

Crime

There is plenty to discuss here. The rules relating to *mens rea*, especially for murder, are problematic. The attempt to achieve justice has left the law uncertain and arguably unjust. Crimes of strict liability allow a criminal conviction without proof of *mens rea*. This seems unjust so if the Act is silent the courts will presume *mens rea* is needed, as in **Sweet v Parsley**. In **Gemmell & Richards**, the HL used the **1966 Practice Statement** to overrule their earlier decision on recklessness in order to achieve justice.

The defence of necessity is rare, but is based on the utilitarian concept of the greater good. In **Re A (conjoined twins) 2000**, the operation to separate conjoined twins (Mary and Jodie) would lead to the death of Mary. Without the operation both twins would die, so it could be argued that her death was justified to bring about the 'greater good' of life for Jodie. The operation was allowed. The opening quote came from this case, recognising that justice means different things to different people.

Theft is a crime whatever is stolen, so if a mother steals milk for her baby she is still guilty of theft. Some people may think the law is unjust, although everyone is being treated equally. However, if each case is decided on its own facts it creates uncertainty. Justice may be achieved during the sentencing stage, rather than by deciding it is not theft.

In **Brown 1994**, on consent to harm, Lord Lowry said sadomasochism was *"not conducive to the welfare of society"*, so a utilitarian might agree with the verdict. The rights of the individuals to consent to harm were outweighed by the effect on society. What do you think Mill would have thought of that?

Task 5 Case study on Re A 2000

Jodie and Mary were born with the lower ends of their spines fused. Mary's heart and lungs did not function and her blood supply was provided by Jodie. Without an operation to separate them, both twins would die, probably within a year or two. Mary could die earlier meaning doctors would have to perform emergency surgery to separate Jodie (with a much lower chance of success). If surgery was performed immediately, Jodie would have a very good chance of a full life; however, Mary would die because she would no longer have the blood supply from Jodie. The hospital wanted to perform the operation and sought approval from the courts.

The parents opposed surgery on religious grounds. They believed that it was not God's will for one child to die to save the other. There were very strong views about morals, justice and conflicting interests in this case. The CA decided that on balance the right to life for Jodie overrode the right to a short and possibly non-existent life for Mary. Ward LJ recognised the problem and said, "Everyone seems to have a view of the proper outcome. I am very well aware of the inevitability that our answer will be applauded by some but that as many will be offended by it"

> **How do you think a utilitarian would decide this case?**
>
> **The parents did not feel they received justice, what do you think?**
>
> **Can you find support for your answer in one of the theories of justice?**
>
> **Do you think the law should be involved in such difficult moral issues?**
>
> **Where there is conflict between parents and doctors who should make the final decision?**
>
> **What problem did Ward LJ recognise?**

Contract

The law tries to achieve a balance between allowing people freedom to make agreements in their own way and protecting the individual against those with more power, who may try to exploit this freedom. The **Unfair Contract Terms Act** limits a business's right to exclude liability. Terms are implied into contracts by both statutes and the courts to protect weaker parties (e.g., **Sale of Goods Act / SOGSA / UCTA / UCTTR / The Moorcock**).

Innominate terms, as seen in **Hong Kong Fir**, are an attempt to achieve justice by focusing on the result of a breach, rather than on the term itself.

In deciding whether something is a term or a representation, the courts will take into account any specialist knowledge in order to do justice to both parties (**Oscar Chess Ltd**).

Equity is based on fairness and can be seen as a higher source of law. Thus, equitable remedies, such as rescission, will only be granted if injustice won't be caused.

Tort

In **Hill v Chief Constable of West Yorkshire**, the police owed no duty of care because it could detract from their overall effectiveness. The individual's right (to damages) was outweighed by the benefit to the public. This is a utilitarian argument.

In **Miller v Jackson**, the utility argument can also be seen. The public benefit of cricket outweighed the individual nuisance and no injunction was granted.

Rylands v Fletcher is a tort of strict liability, which makes a person liable without proof of fault. This can be seen as unjust.

The decision that a learner driver is expected to reach the standard of a competent driver could be seen as unjust in **Nettleship v Weston**. However, the driver was best able to bear the cost, through her insurance company.

The defence of contributory negligence allows the court to apportion liability in a way that seeks to achieve justice. Use any cases on this defence to discuss this. A recent example is **Belka v Prosperini 2011**. C had drunk about four pints of beer and he was hit by a taxi while he and a friend were crossing a dual carriageway near a roundabout. He claimed in negligence for his injuries. The court found that both the taxi-driver and C were to blame. Justice was achieved by apportioning blame so that C received compensation, but this was reduced according to his level of fault. Similarly, in **Sedge v Prime 2011**, C had been drinking and stepped out onto a narrow road without looking. He was hit by a car and suffered serious injuries. The driver was found to be in breach of his duty of care to a pedestrian because he was in a 20 mph limit zone where there were several pubs and fast-food outlets, and it was 'turning out' time for the pubs. The driver was found to be 75% responsible. Justice here was achieved by finding the driver mostly responsible because his was the greater fault, but also finding that C had a 25% share of the blame because had he looked he would have seen the car.

Also on defences, consent is only available where it is real consent, thus in **Smith v Baker**, the court protected the weaker party (the employee) by finding there was no true consent.

Contemporary issues

The **Protection of Freedoms Act 2012** repealed s 43 of the **Criminal Justice Act 2003** which allowed complex fraud trials to be heard without a jury. However, it does not affect **s44** which allows for trial without jury where there are fears of jury tampering. The first trial without jury in a major criminal case took place in January 2010, due to fear that the jury could be 'nobbled'. It has long been argued that justice must not only be done, but also be seen to be done, and that a trial by one's peers is a major pillar in the legal justice system. Protestors outside the court held placards reading "No jury. No justice". In March 2014 the Lord Chief Justice, Lord Thomas again raised the suggestion that the right to trial by jury should be removed for minor offences and fraud trials. The debate is clearly a continuing one.

The **Protection of Freedoms Act 2012** reduces the detention of terrorist suspects to a maximum of 14 days without charge. It further provides that fingerprint and DNA evidence must be destroyed following a decision not to charge or an acquittal in court. These issues had often been cited as unjust and have been the subject of various campaigns and protests.

In **HJ (Iran) v Home Department 2010**, the Supreme Court ruled that gay and lesbian asylum seekers should not be forced to return to a country where they will be persecuted. The Government had said that they could avoid persecution by pretending to be heterosexual. The Supreme Court said this was to deny them their fundamental rights to be who they are.

In **Gilderdale 2010**, a woman who killed her daughter in an assisted suicide was found not guilty of murder by the jury and given a 12-month conditional discharge. The judge said the decision of the jury showed "common sense, decency and humanity". Many agreed with the judge and thought justice was done, but many others thought that justice was not done because she had taken a life. In **Inglis 2010**, in similar circumstances, the mother was sentenced to life because she was found guilty of murder. The contrast in sentencing in these cases shows the difficulty in having a mandatory life sentence. Once murder is established the judge has no discretion, so Mrs Inglis was given life even though it was accepted she acted in what she believed were her son's best interests although (unlike Mrs Gilderdale's daughter) he was unable to communicate his wishes. Justice demands that there is greater consistency in the law.

Task 6

Look at the cases of **Inglis** and **Gilderdale** and answer the following questions.

1. The conviction in **Inglis** was for murder rather than assisted suicide, as was the case in **Gilderdale**. Can you see a problem with this?
2. Do you think justice was done in these two cases?
3. How would these decisions be viewed by a natural law theorist?

In **Edwards v Environment Agency (Cemex UK Cement Co Ltd intervening) 2011**, a question arose regarding the powers of the Supreme Court. The SC confirmed that it had all the powers previously invested in the House of Lords. This included the power to correct any injustice caused by an earlier decision of the House or the Supreme Court, however it might have arisen. This confirmed that the powers given to the HL under the **1966 Practice Statement** have passed to the SC, so earlier decisions can be overruled in the interests of justice.

The **Legal Aid, Sentencing and Punishment of Offenders Act 2012** came into force in April 2013. This restricts access to justice for many people. It removes legal aid from numerous cases such as most personal injury claims, which means people will have to use the 'no win, no fee system'. This has also been changed so that the claimant not the losing party now pays the success fee (up to 25% of the amount awarded). The concerns surrounding the denial of justice meant the legislation had a rocky ride through Parliament. The bill was defeated and amended several times in the House of Lords and after nearly eleven months – and an extended session of 'Ping-Pong' at the end – was eventually passed on a tied vote (which means a government victory). The arguments against the bill were that any system of justice should be based on equality and that if people felt they could not get access to justice they would not believe in the rule of law. The bill was seen as an example of inequality before the law and a poor example of distributive justice. However, the Minister of Justice argued that although legal aid is "an essential part of the justice system" the money has to come from taxpayers and resources are limited.

Examination tip

Read the question carefully. You may be asked for a general discussion, and/or to consider a specific question, e.g., "How far does the law *promote* justice"? Parliament can attempt to *promote* justice by making particular rules. In contract, various Acts give protection to consumers. In tort, the **Occupier's Liability Act 1984** protects people even though they may have no right to be on someone's land. It was the attempt to do justice in **BRB v Herrington** that led to this Act being passed. Similarly, following the **Quintavalle** case Parliament passed the **Human Fertilisation and Embryology Act 2008**. This shows that case law can also promote justice by highlighting any gaps or uncertainties in the law and encouraging the government to make changes through Parliament.

Sentencing and remedies can also promote justice, e.g., by deterrence and by making people act more carefully in future.

Not only do the theorists differ in their ideas of justice, so do most ordinary people. In a televised report of a court case, you often see pictures of the families and friends of both the victim and the accused outside the court, all demanding 'justice'. Whatever the outcome of the case, it is unlikely that they all think they got it.

The case of the Libyan, Al Megrahi, convicted of the 1988 'Lockerbie bombing' over Scotland, reflects the different ways people view 'justice'. In 2009, he was allowed by the Scottish government to return to Libya, as he was ill and expected to die within a few months. (He actually died in 2012.) The Americans who had family killed on the flight were strongly opposed to the decision to allow him to return to Libya to die, and wished to see him punished in full for his actions – retributive justice. The Scottish families said they wanted a full enquiry to establish the facts of the case, as many of them remain unconvinced of his guilt. Justice to them meant ensuring that the man accused was actually guilty.

Essay pointer

What do you think the families and friends actually mean when they say they want justice? Look out for stories in the press. As you read them, ask yourself whether 'justice' has been achieved. Then consider whether any of the above theorists would have agreed. Finally, ask the all-important question, "justice for whom?" Write some notes on this to keep as material for revision and essay practice.

Examination tip

Examiners are looking for independence of thought so you need to develop your own ideas. Use some of the examples given here but don't just cite them. Pick out a few and see how well you can explain them. Include references to some of the theories and possibly add other cases to illustrate. Try to include something current that involves a question of promoting or achieving justice.

Example

Re A is a good example of the difficulties judges face when trying to achieve justice. The parents and the doctors could not agree and nor would the theorists. A follower of natural law would want to uphold the parents' wishes, as the operation would kill one of the twins and taking a life is immoral and therefore not justice. A utilitarian would say that overall the most benefits would be achieved by the operation going ahead because at least one life would be saved, however the effect on society as a whole would need to be taken into account. Many people would argue that justice is better achieved by the law coming from an elected Parliament rather than from judges. The same can be said for the law on assisted suicide and euthanasia where many cases such as **Purdy**, **Nicklinson** and **Gilderdale**, have come before the courts because Parliament is reluctant to act. Justice cannot be achieved if the law is not clear.

Task 7

Choose a case, Act or procedure and write a paragraph about whether it achieves justice, as in the above example

Summary

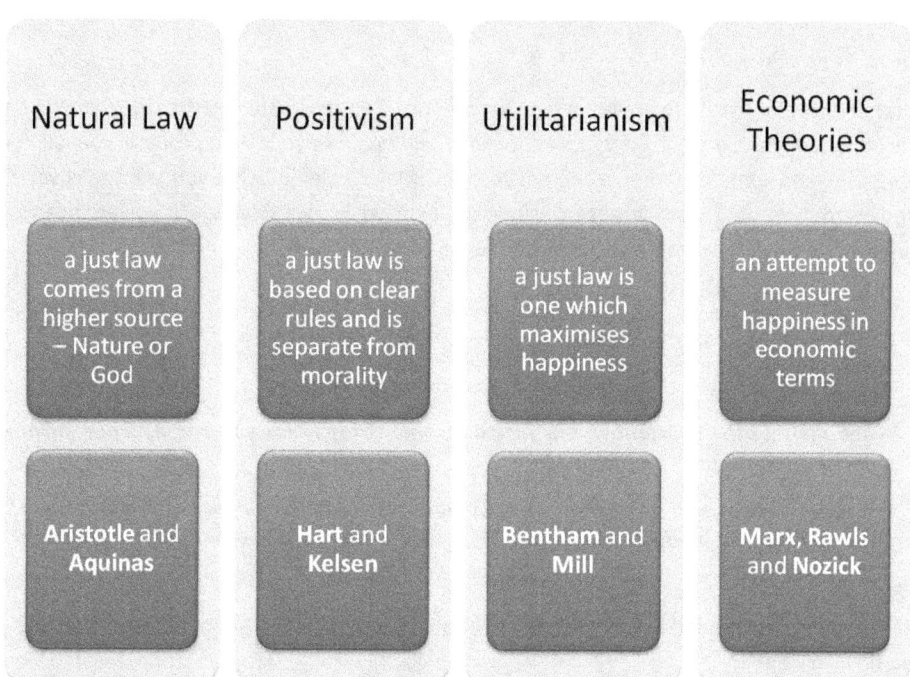

Natural Law	Positivism	Utilitarianism	Economic Theories
a just law comes from a higher source – Nature or God	a just law is based on clear rules and is separate from morality	a just law is one which maximises happiness	an attempt to measure happiness in economic terms
Aristotle and **Aquinas**	**Hart** and **Kelsen**	**Bentham** and **Mill**	**Marx, Rawls** and **Nozick**

Self-test questions

What is the Utilitarian theory based on?

What do positivists attempt to separate?

What did Mill add to Utilitarianism?

Where does Natural Law come from?

Apply one of these theories to any case of your choice.

A general guide to revision

The first and foremost rule for revision is to start early. Too many students leave it until the last minute and then get in a panic. If you take it gently and organise your time properly you will feel a lot more calm and confident when exam time comes. Make a plan of what you want to cover each day and try to stick to it. Don't forget to include some breaks in your schedule, if you are tired it will be harder to retain the material you have been revising.

Here are a few tips for revision techniques

> *Go through your notes and try to summarise them*
>
> *Be sure you understand any problems a case raises or solves*
>
> *When revising the substantive law pick out some cases which you can also use for one or more of the concepts*
>
> *Learn these cases well so that you can evaluate them with confidence and relate them to a particular concept of law*

Example

In **Brown**, the judges decided that consent was not a defence to serious harm, so this would apply to a scenario involving GBH.

It raises a problem in the law, because the reasoning was obscure. It was not sufficiently clear why the consent defence failed. It could be argued that the defence fails if harm was intended (this would apply to **s 18** but not **s 20**), or alternatively that the defence fails if harm was serious (this would apply to both **s 18** and **s 20**).

Another problem, and one which relates to the concepts of law and morals and law and justice, is that some judges seemed to rely on their own moral values when reaching their decision. According to the positivist view of justice, law and morals should be kept separate.

> *Go through the summaries of the topic. These provide a base of the essential points which may need to be addressed*
>
> *Go to the examination board's website for past exam papers, mark schemes and reports*
>
> *Practise answering questions then look at the examiners' mark schemes and reports to see if you were on the right track*

Revision of Law and Justice

Natural Law considers a just law as coming from a higher source

> The source of law is above us so we should obey it
>
> Only law based on moral rules must be obeyed
>
> There is distributive justice and corrective justice

Positivism considers law as coming from those authorised to make law (Parliament or the courts)

> If a law is made correctly by those in authority, we must obey it, regardless of any moral content

If we do not obey it, sanctions will follow (corrective justice)

Procedural justice looks at whether the legal process is just; substantive justice looks at whether the law itself is just

Utilitarianism considers justice as based on the consequences of the law

Justice is achieved by a law that produces the maximum benefit for the greatest number

Individual rights are unimportant; the law is just as long as the majority benefit

Libertarian and egalitarian theories developed utilitarianism to consider quality of life not just quantity

Mill thought people should be free to choose what they do unless it causes harm to others

Law should only prohibit activities that harm others, rather than behaviour that is immoral or offensive

Economic theories are based on the distribution of wealth and property (distributive justice)

Rawls saw justice as achieved where wealth and property is fairly distributed by the state – based on equality

Nozick saw justice as achieved where wealth and property is come by fairly – even if this did not produce equality, the state should not intervene

Marx would want the state to intervene to ensure a distribution that shared wealth and property according to need

Example

In **Rogers v Swindon NHS Primary Care Trust**, the problem was one of economics. Hospitals have limited resources and drugs can be expensive. If someone needs costly treatment, should it be made available? Rawls would want to see resources shared equally, which would deny the treatment to an individual. Marx would want any distribution of resources to depend on the needs of the individual patient, but would advocate that the money should come from those able to pay (*"from each according to his ability, to each according to his needs"*). In both views, the state should intervene to ensure a just distribution. However, in practice resources are limited so it will be difficult to achieve justice for all.

Task 8

Give two examples of a legal process that promotes justice. Don't forget to include examples and/or theories to illustrate.

Examination practice

A general guide to examination papers

Read **all** questions carefully before deciding which to answer.

Look again at the ones you wish to answer to make sure you can do so, make brief notes – this can be a useful checklist later when you are tired and your memory begins to fail.

Structure your answer. A solid start is worth a lot and gets the examiner on your side. A small plan is helpful.

It is necessary to do more than regurgitate your notes. Never put in irrelevant material just because you know it – there is **never** a question asking you to 'write all you know about...'. You need to be selective as to what is relevant, and choose appropriate cases and examples in support of what you say.

In essay questions, you will usually be asked to form an opinion or to weigh up arguments for and against a particular statement. Here a broader range of knowledge is needed showing arguments for, arguments against and an evaluation of these arguments. You should always round off your answer with a short concluding paragraph, preferably using some of the wording from the question to indicate to the examiner that you are addressing the specific issue raised.

Essays should have a logical structure. The beginning should introduce the subject matter, the central part should explain/analyse/criticise it as appropriate, and the conclusion should bring the various strands of argument together with reference to the question set.

Try to consider alternative arguments. A well-rounded essay will bring in other views even if you disagree with them; you cannot shoot them down without setting them up first.

Essay writing is a skill in itself, so here is a brief guide on how to structure your essay.

Writing a discussion essay: staging the information logically

If you stage your essay as follows, it will make it easy to read, logically structured and easier to write. It may also mean you don't leave out important points. Here's how it works:

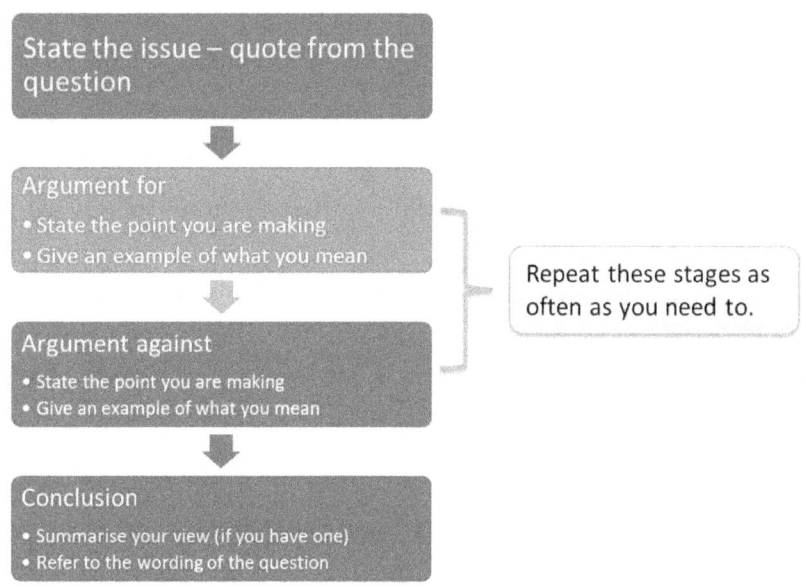

Writing each paragraph: making each one logical and easy to read (and write!)

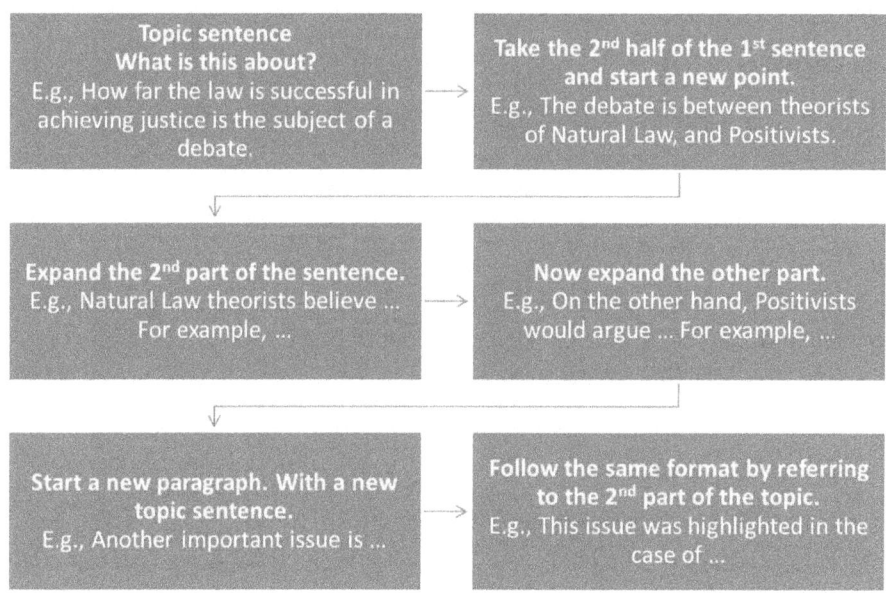

Finally, make sure you cover the whole question; there are only a certain number of marks available. The examiner has a mark scheme to work to, so however brilliant your answer to one part of the question is, missing out the other parts will severely reduce your total marks.

Examination practice for Law and Justice

Although different exam boards have different ways of styling their examination papers, there are always going to be common elements. You will need to be able to evaluate a given concept to provide a critique of the area, including case examples and reference to theorists where appropriate.

Many exam boards suggest you should use current issues and developments in the law when answering questions on jurisprudence or concepts of law. Keep an eye on current affairs and try to bring in some of your own ideas as to how far the law achieves justice and/or the difficulties of doing so. As stated earlier, there is no right answer to these issues but if you offer your own view avoid being too opinionated. Remember this is a law exam, so always use the theories, cases, Acts of Parliament and/or legal procedures to support what you say.

As with law and morals there are several matters which may arise in questions about law and justice, these include:

Discussion of the different possible meanings of justice e.g. in terms of basic fairness or equality of treatment

Distinction between different aspects of justice e.g. distributive/corrective, substantive/procedural

Discussion of the philosophical theories of justice e.g., natural law, positivism and utilitarianism, economic theories)

In addition, there will be a specific point raised by the question these could include:

The relationship between law and justice

Whether and/or how far the law achieves justice

Whether it is reasonable to expect the law to do so

The difficulties in doing so

These latter points will require an evaluation based on the earlier discussion, with cases and examples in support.

The 'Essay pointers' and 'Tasks' provide you with information to use in an essay. Look through these before doing the examination practice tasks below.

Examination tip

An important point made by examiners is that it is not enough to decide a law or case or procedure is unjust, you need to connect it to a particular description of justice, e.g., that it does not accord with equality, corrective justice, Utilitarianism etc.

A brief review of what you should consider before attempting an essay question.

Essays should have a logical structure

The beginning – should introduce the subject matter

The central part – should explain/analyse/criticise it as appropriate with examples and alternative arguments

The conclusion – should bring the various strands of argument together with reference to the question set

The following two tasks will give you a basis for an essay on law and justice.

Task 9 examination practice

Using some of the examples in the table, write an essay (around 400 words) on the statement below it, taken from an exam paper. Include some reference to the theories or debates surrounding the particular area.

Statement: Consider how far the law is able to achieve justice.

A possible focus of an examination question would be to ask you to discuss the difficulties which the law faces in seeking to achieve justice. Write a paragraph (350 to 400 words) highlighting one or two of these difficulties and using a logical structure.

There is no 'right' answer to evaluation questions, opinions vary and you can form your own – but **always** use cases and/or examples to back up what you say.

This is an example of a typical examination question.

Critically discuss the different possible meanings of justice and discuss the difficulties which the law faces in achieving justice.

Answers to self-test questions and tasks

Mill believed the law should not be involved unless harm is likely to be caused to others. He may have agreed with the law against drinking and driving because drinking and driving can seriously harm other road users. It is less likely he would agree with the law making seat belts compulsory as not wearing a seat belt is unlikely to harm anyone but the person concerned, so it should be a matter of personal choice.

Task 2

This depends on your chosen case. An example would be **Donoghue v Stevenson**. This case set a precedent that allowed a consumer to sue a negligent manufacturer even though there was not contract between them (because she had not bought the ginger beer herself). This allowed justice to be done not only for the individual (Mrs Donoghue) but also for all consumers. The new law achieved the greatest overall benefit for society because people received better protection and the manufacturers could avoid liability by taking greater care, or they could have insurance in place to meet the costs of compensation. A utilitarian would see this law as just.

Task 3

The CA quashed the decision because it felt that exceptional circumstances should be based on clinical needs rather than personal matters. The CA's point was not that all treatment should be funded, but that the policy in relation to funding should be fairer and more transparent.

A utilitarian would probably argue that the money would be better spent on care for a greater number of patients.

The utilitarian approach ignores the needs of the individual patient and looks at the needs of society as a whole. Mill might say that the law should not be involved unless harm will be caused to others. However, it can be said that harm is caused either to the person denied treatment, or to other patients who would be denied treatment if one patient received an expensive drug. This means the law is right to get involved.

There is no right answer to such questions. The individual would be better off but other patients may lose out if funds dry up. If treatment is expensive and funds have to be allocated from limited resources, this will reduce what is available for other patients.

You could say that it should be up to the hospital or Trust to decide what they can afford and the law should not interfere. However, if someone like Mrs Rogers challenges a decision someone has to arbitrate.

If decisions were made on a case-by-case basis, depending on available funds, then arguably the system would be unclear and inconsistent, so justice would not be achieved. Justice requires equal treatment and fairness and if it was up to the individual Trust whether to provide treatment or not, then perhaps justice will not be achieved. A situation may arise which has become known as a 'postcode lottery' for treatment. This means people in one area receive treatment that those in another area are denied. It is arguable that justice cannot be achieved in such a system.

Task 4

The first theory is positivism

The second theory is utilitarianism

The third theory is natural law

Task 5

A utilitarian would argue that to achieve the greatest benefit for the greatest number the operation should be allowed because Mary would die with or without it, whereas Jodie had a far higher chance of a healthy life if the operation took place.

This is a matter of opinion. It can be argued that the parents should be the ones to decide such a personal issue as this. On the other hand, if the operation did not take place Jodie may well have died and she deserved justice too.

This depends on your previous answer. As seen above, a utilitarian would argue for the operation to take place but a follower of natural law is more likely to see the taking of Mary's life as immoral and therefore unjust.

Again, this is a matter of opinion. If the people concerned do not agree then someone has to make a decision, and arguably justice is better served by a judge deciding the issue. However, in cases such as this, one party will clearly believe that justice has not been achieved.

There is no 'right' answer to this. The doctors are probably in a better position to make the decision based on medical and scientific knowledge rather than emotion and/or religion. However, it is difficult to argue that parents should not be allowed to decide something that involves the life and death of their children. Those opposed to the operation regarded life as sacrosanct and believed the law should not intervene to allow the operation. Those in favour regarded the fact that Jodie would have a good chance of a long and healthy life as being paramount and that, sad though it was, the loss of Mary's life was inevitable with or without the operation, so it was better to perform it.

Ward LJ recognised that some people would agree and others disagree with the decision. This case is a very good example of the difficulties judges face in trying to achieve justice.

Task 6

The problem is that murder carries a mandatory life sentence, so the judge has no discretion and cannot consider the particular circumstances. This means the law makes no distinction between cases of euthanasia and 'cold-blooded' murder (as was pointed out by the chief executive of Dignity in Dying).

There is no right answer and opinions will differ. In both cases, the woman took a life so it can be argued that jail was a fitting punishment. On this view then maybe justice was achieved in the **Inglis** case, but not in **Gilderdale** where she walked free. However, a more liberal argument would be that that justice was not achieved in **Inglis**, as the judge could not take into account that she acted in what she believed were her son's best interests. The sentence for murder can only be life imprisonment. Clearly, Mrs Inglis should not have taken the law into her own hands, especially as her son had no way of stating his own wishes, but the huge difference in punishment between the two women can be seen as unjust. With Mrs Gilderdale, the jury acquitted her so she walked free from court. If she had not already admitted to, and been convicted of, aiding a suicide she would have no criminal record. It can be argued that even though she acted in her daughter's best interests, the evidence was that she had intended to kill and so prison would be a just result. Whatever the reasons, she had taken a life. However, juries are reluctant to convict in such circumstance because they know that there is only one possible sentence. Arguably, if the sentence was at the judge's discretion there may well have been a conviction by the jury. They would know that the judge could consider the circumstances when sentencing, and so attempt to achieve justice at that stage. At the very least there would be unlikely to be such a huge disparity between the two cases regarding the sentence.

A natural law theorist is likely to see the decision in **Gilderdale** as wrong because, whatever her reasons, her actions in taking a life were immoral and so justice was not done. The decision in **Inglis** would more likely be viewed as a correct one, achieving justice based on the moral code of not taking a life.

There will be many different answers to this question depending on what you chose. This is just one example using an Act that also involves legal procedure, with reference to the economic theories of justice.

The **Legal Aid, Sentencing and Punishment of Offenders Act 2012** reduced access to justice for many people. That it was a controversial bill, removing funding from many who needed it and reducing compensation by changing who pays the success fee, can be seen in the length of time it took to go through Parliament and the amendments proposed by the House of Lords but rejected by the Commons. The **Legal Aid Act 1949** and the **Access to Justice Act 1999** made a great many improvements to access to funding and to the courts for a wide range of people who could not otherwise afford their 'day in court'. Many argue the new Act is a backward step but the Minister of Justice said that although legal aid is "an essential part of the justice system" the money has to come from taxpayers and resources are limited. The shadow justice minister said that any system of justice should be based on equality. As an example of distributive justice, it seems to fail. Marx would argue that resources should be distributed according to need and this is no longer the case. Rawls would want an egalitarian distribution and this has failed as well. The shadow justice minister will not see justice as done, because even though the law applies to everyone equally the effect is that poorer people will be the losers and the rich will save their taxes.

Self-test questions

The Utilitarian theory is based on maximising happiness

Positivists attempt to separate law and morals

Mill added individual rights to Utilitarianism

Natural Law comes from God or nature

This depends on your chosen case

One example of the legal process promoting justice is the rules of precedent. Precedent is based on '*stare decisis*', or treating like cases alike, and this rule provides equality and consistency in the law. Other rules can avoid injustice caused by too strict an adherence to this principle, e.g., the **Practice Statement** allows the Supreme Court (formerly the House of Lords) to overrule its own earlier decisions in the interests of justice. An example of this is **Gemmell & Richards** where the House of Lords used the **Practice Statement** to change the law on recklessness for criminal damage. This is a form of what Aristotle called corrective justice. The injustice of finding the boys guilty of a crime when they did not recognise the risk of their actions was corrected by the later decision. All recklessness is now subjective and this applies equally to anyone accused of a crime where the *mens rea* is recklessness.

Another example of a legal process that promotes justice is existence of the Criminal Cases Review Commission set up in 1995. This Commission was set up with the sole purpose of correcting injustice. An example is **Kennedy 2007** where the CCRC returned the case to the Court of Appeal where his conviction for manslaughter was overturned. Again, this illustrates corrective justice.

In a civilised world the law can, and should, attempt to achieve justice but we live in a complex society so perhaps it is unrealistic to expect it to do so all the time. Conflicting views of what amounts to justice in a particular case show the difficulties; there is never a 'justice for all' and this was highlighted in the case of **Re A**.

What may seem just to Utilitarians might not appear just to supporters of Natural law. Utilitarians might argue that the law was applied unjustly in **Purdy** because she was disadvantaged, and yet no one else benefited. Supporters of natural law on the other hand would argue that the sanctity of life is a fundamental principle, which cannot be compromised. It cannot be just to go against the 'higher law', therefore the decision was just. One theory of justice is that of equality, but Ms Purdy was treated equally when she wanted to be treated as an individual case. She did not feel that justice was achieved, so perhaps treating people equally does not always achieve justice. In **Purdy** and **Quintavalle** there were strong conflicting arguments from pressure groups about whether justice was achieved, showing the difficulties in achieving justice. On one view it is more just to uphold the fundamental principle of the sanctity of life, on the other hand it is arguably not just to refuse a person freedom of choice over life and death, if that is what they want, as Mill would argue. Similarly, in **Brown,** it was not just that they had their freedoms restricted when acting in private. Mill would support Ms Purdy as he advocated freedom of choice as long as others were not harmed, it is less clear that he would have supported the defendants in **Brown** as harm was caused. The conflicting decisions in **Brown** and **Wilson** show the law has less chance of achieving justice when it is influenced by the morality of the act. It will be difficult to achieve justice if different standards are applied in such cases, especially if one considers justice as equality of treatment. **Cox** and **Bland** are other cases that are hard to reconcile. Giving a lethal injection at a patient's request led to a murder charge in **Cox**, but in **Bland**, withdrawing artificial feeding was seen as an omission and so not unlawful. It is hard to say that justice is done when such a fine line is drawn. After considering the difficulties the law faces, it is not surprising that there are limits to the extent to which it achieves justice.

There are many difficulties which you could discuss. Here are a couple of possibilities.

The difficulty of the law achieving justice is particularly acute in procedural law. Hart referred to procedural justice as 'justice according to law' and this means considering whether the legal process is just. Access to justice, the right to appeal and jury trials are all examples of an attempt to achieve justice by increasing equality before the law. These have met with varying degrees of success. For example, although the law has attempted to provide better access to justice with the **Legal Aid Act** and the **Access to Justice Act**, there are still difficulties with achieving justice for all. Later reductions in legal aid have weakened a defendant's right to a fair trial, and a claimant's right to take a case to court. Although there are some alternative schemes for civil cases, such as 'no win, no fee', the **Legal Aid, Sentencing and Punishment of Offenders Act 2012** has reduced access to justice for numerous people by removing funding from many who needed it and reducing compensation by changing who pays the success fee. A failure of the legal system to provide justice for everyone results in inequality and therefore injustice.

However, it is difficult for the law to provide justice to everyone because justice means different things to different people. For a utilitarian, justice would mean providing the greatest benefit for the majority, but this can lead to injustice for individuals, as can be seen in the anti-terrorism laws. The number of days a suspected terrorist can be detained without charge was reduced to 14 days by the **Protection of Freedoms Act 2012**, but as the Law Society said about the earlier law, *"it is essential that emergency terror legislation protects the country without compromising the government's duty to uphold fairness and justice".* This is an example of the difficulties in achieving justice for everyone, because everyone wants to be safe but no one wants to be locked up without charge. Laws that allow for detention without charge are arguably against natural law because they conflict with the fundamental rule that no one should be imprisoned without a fair trial. This is especially true in a country where a person is supposed to be 'innocent until proved guilty' in a court of law. Overall, it can be said that there has been some success in achieving justice but difficulties remain.

Task 11

Here is a plan of how to approach an essay. Use the answers to all the tasks, especially tasks 7, 8, 9 and 10, to see how you could develop some of these points.

The theories can be brought into either part. If used in the first then you can refer back to them in the second.

You won't have time to cover everything so select those examples that makes sense to you. There may be a need to strike a balance between breadth and depth. As long as the answer is not superficial, and – most importantly – covers the specific question, a candidate who covers a greater number of theories and/or examples would be expected to do so in less detail.

> *Discuss the different meanings of justice e.g. in terms of fairness or equality*
>
> *Discuss the theories of justice e.g., natural law, positivism, utilitarianism, economic theories*
>
> *Distinguish between different aspects of justice e.g. distributive/corrective, substantive/procedural (Aristotle/Hart)*
>
> *Discuss the need for distributive justice to achieve equality, e.g., access to justice, legal funding, consumer law*
>
> *Discuss the need for corrective justice to ensure any injustice is put right, e.g., the CCRC, sentencing and remedies*
>
> *Discuss the need for justice in the substantive law, e.g., consumer protection and anti-discrimination laws to balance inequalities*
>
> *Discuss the need for a just system of procedural law to ensure equality and fairness, e.g., access to justice and legal funding, jury trials, the rule of precedent to treat like cases alike*
>
> *Discuss the need for the law to help balance conflicting interests between parties to a dispute in order to achieve justice*
>
> *Explain and evaluate the difficulties in achieving justice, these include*
>
>> *The difficulty of providing justice in light of the disagreement as to what justice is with reference to the debates between natural law, positivism and utilitarianism*
>>
>> *The problem of distributive justice as regards what is a fair distribution, with reference to the economic theories*

The difficulty of achieving justice in substantive law and balancing competing interests satisfactorily in a complex and multi-cultural society, e.g., anti-terrorism laws, Re A, Quintavalle etc.

The difficulty of reconciling utilitarian theories with individual rights (Bentham/Mill)

Provide a conclusion referring to the difficulties

It is important in an examination to finish with a strong concluding paragraph. This should briefly sum up your arguments referring to the wording of the question, e.g., to the word 'difficulties' here, this will show the examiner that you have addressed the specific point raised.

Example

"Although several laws have been created which address inequality and injustice to some extent, in particular with consumer protection and anti-discrimination laws, it can be said that the legal system has failed to provide justice for everyone. Such inequality inevitably results in injustice. However, it is difficult for the law to achieve justice for everyone because justice means different things to different people. For a utilitarian justice would mean providing the greatest benefit for the majority, but this can lead to injustice for individuals, as can be seen in **Rogers** *and in the anti-terrorism laws. Overall, it can be said that difficulties in achieving justice will always remain while there are disagreements on what justice actually means."*

Examination tip

Cases where the parties involved disagree, or where society itself is divided on the issue, will always be useful in illustrating the difficulties of achieving justice for all. There are plenty of examples above, but look at your notes on 'Law and Morals' too. Many of the cases there will highlight the difficulties because where there is a moral element to the law there is rarely agreement on whether justice has been achieved.

Appendix: Abbreviations and acknowledgements

The following abbreviations are commonly used. You may use them in an examination answer, but write them in full the first time, e.g., write 'actual bodily harm (ABH)' and then after that, you can just write 'ABH'.

General

Draft Code – A Criminal Code for England and Wales (Law Commission No. 177), 1989

CCRC Criminal Cases Review Commission

ABH actual bodily harm

GBH grievous bodily harm

D defendant

C claimant

V Victim

CA Court of Appeal

HL House of Lords

SC Supreme Court

Acts

S – section (thus **s 1** Theft Act 1968 refers to section 1 of that Act)

s 1(2) means section 1 subsection 2 of an Act.

OAPA – Offences against the Person Act 1861

In cases – these don't need to be written in full

CC (at beginning) chief constable

CC (at end) county council

BC borough council

DC district council

LBC London borough council

AHA Area Health Authority

J Justice

LJ Lord Justice

LCJ Lord Chief Justice

LC Lord Chancellor

AG Attorney General

CPS Crown Prosecution Service

DPP Director of Public Prosecutions

AG Attorney General

Acknowledgements

I am grateful to the following for examination questions.

The Assessment and Qualification Alliance (AQA)

Note: Where worked solutions to, and/or commentaries on, AQA questions or possible answers are provided it is the author who is responsible for them. They have not been provided or approved by AQA and do not necessarily constitute the only possible solutions.

I am also grateful to my husband, Dave, for many hours of proof reading and for his hard work on the diagrams.

www.ingramcontent.com/pod-product-compliance
Lightning Source LLC
Chambersburg PA
CBHW070733180526
45167CB00004B/1741